Tw~'
abou

ex libris

Candlestick Press

Published by:
Candlestick Press,
Diversity House, 72 Nottingham Road, Arnold, Nottingham NG5 6LF
www.candlestickpress.co.uk

Design, typesetting, print and production by Diversity Creative
Marketing Solutions Ltd., www.diversity.agency

Introduction © Pippa Greenwood, 2015

Illustrations, including cover © Beth Krommes, 2015
www.bethkrommes.com

© Candlestick Press, 2015

ISBN 978 1 907598 33 3

Donation to British Hen Welfare Trust www.bhwt.org.uk

Acknowledgements:
Our thanks to Jean Atkin for permission to reprint 'March Araucana', first
published in *The Henkeeper's Almanac* (Biscuit Tin Press, 2013). Thanks
also to Diana Gittins and Happen*Stance* Press for permission to reprint
her untitled poem from *Bork!* (Happen*Stance* Press, 2013). Caroline
Hawkridge's poem 'Cockerel' first appeared in *The Interpreter's House 55*
and is printed here by kind permission of the author. Jacqueline Brown's
poem 'Scrambled' is reprinted from *Thinking Egg* (Littlewood Arc, 1993)
by kind permission of the publisher. 'Doubt' by Kay Ryan is from *Elephant
Rocks* copyright © 1996 by Kay Ryan and is used by permission of Grove/
Atlantic, Inc. Any third party use of this material, outside of this publication,
is prohibited. Robert Frost, 'A Blue Ribbon at Amesbury', is reprinted from
The Poetry of Robert Frost (Jonathan Cape, 1971) by kind permission of
the Random House Group and, in North America, Henry Holt & Co. Jane
Sudworth's poem 'Hatching' from *A Pocketful of Windows* (Valley Press,
2014) is reprinted here by kind permission of the author and publisher.
'Fingers in the Nesting Box' by Robert Graves, is reprinted by permission of
Carcanet Press and first appeared in Robert Graves, *The Complete Poems in
One Volume*, (Carcanet Press, 2000). Norman MacCaig, 'Cock before dawn',
was first published in *Poems of Norman MacCaig* (Polygon, 2005) and is
reprinted by kind permission of Berlinn Ltd. Gary Whitehead, 'A Glossary of
Chickens', was first published in his collection of the same name (Princeton
University Press, 2013) and is reprinted by kind permission of Princeton
University Press.

While every effort has been made to secure permission to reprint material
protected by copyright, we will be pleased to make good any omissions
brought to our attention in future printings of this pamphlet

Where poets are no longer living, their dates are given.

Contents

Introduction

I've always hankered after hens and when we moved to our present house, nearly twenty years ago, I was able to take the plunge. Over the years we have been lucky enough to have our lives graced with numerous hens; initially a few 'posh' birds, then an unwanted rooster joined us from a friend's house.... so fertile eggs soon followed, some of which we hatched in a borrowed incubator. I'll never forget seeing those tiny chicks burst forth – a mesmerising experience watched by the entire family, both our tiny kids plucked from their beds to watch something they too will never forget.

A few years ago I was working at a garden show and there opposite me were the lovely people from The British Hen Welfare Trust, complete with a few somewhat moth-eaten hens. By the end of those few days I knew that the time had come to re-home some hens who would otherwise have been destined for death. Armed with cardboard boxes and a cat basket my son and I picked up our first rescue hens. There began a truly wonderful experience. It has really changed us to watch those girls experience real life for the first time, to witness that first attempt at scratching up soil (the hen watched fascinated as her leg began to scratch....I cried!) to witness their enormous enthusiasm for everything, their unbeatable lust for life and to have the chance to see them re-feather, perk up and develop un-stoppable characters and very individual habits. We always knew we liked hens, we have always tended towards re-cycled/re-homed/rescue animals but these BHWT ginger girlies have melted all our hearts. Forget 'friends' on social media sites, I have a FLOCK of fabulous friends who run to greet me whenever I'm in the garden....though perhaps even more enthusiastically when I'm carrying anything yellow (which might, just possibly, be sweetcorn!!).

Pippa Greenwood

More about Pippa on her website www.pippagreenwood.com

Cockerel

There you stand: a weather-vane
with one foot held up as if you could pluck
East and West from the very ends
of the earth. You splay
the yellow crackle-glaze of your toes and step
forward, eyeing me with a shiny bit
you might have pecked
from the dust.

The fleshy rinds on your head
make a ramshackle bouquet
when you elongate your neck, part
that kettle beak and start to pour yourself out
and out; the undulating effort travelling
the muscles of your throat as if
you can rouse the world

from its shell of cloud
and molten
yolk.

Caroline Hawkridge

A Glossary Of Chickens

There should be a word for the way
they look with just one eye, neck bent
for beetle or worm or strewn grain.
"Gleaning", maybe, between *"gizzard"*
and *"grit."* And for the way they run
toward someone they trust, their skirts
hiked, their plump bodies wobbling:
"bobbling," let's call it, inserted
after *"blowout"* and before *"bloom."*
There should be terms, too, for things
they do not do – like urinate or chew –
but perhaps there already are.
I'd want a word for the way they drink,
head thrown back, throat wriggling,
like an old woman swallowing
a pill; a word beginning with "S,"
coming after *"sex feather"* and before *"shank."*
And one for the sweetness of hens
but not roosters. We think
that by naming we can understand,
as if the tongue were more than muscle.

Gary Whitehead

Hen's Nest

Among the orchard weeds, from every search,
Snugly and sure, the old hen's nest is made,
Who cackles every morning from her perch
To tell the servant girl new eggs are laid;
Who lays her washing by, and far and near
Goes seeking all about from day to day,
And stung with nettles tramples everywhere;
But still the cackling pullet lays away.
The boy on Sundays goes the stack to pull
In hopes to find her there, but naught is seen,
And takes his hat and thinks to find it full,
She's laid so long so many might have been.
But naught is found and all is given o'er
Till the young brood come chirping to the door.

John Clare (1793 – 1864)

Hatching

I will tell you how it is…
after an eternity
of incubation, barely
conscious,
comes the time.

Months of mining,
mole blind,
an inpenetrable wall
with a tiny hammer,
eventually
makes a hole.

You take a single sip
of fresh air, and
become aware of
the impossibility of
your situation.

Trapped
in a womb tomb
tired, tied, now
you must turn and
turn and

persistent

pick and chip to make
a manhole cover:
a trap-door which,
if pushed hard enough,
(and I mean really hard!)

will pop
open
and
with a final,
almighty
struggle, you

flop,

damp and exhausted,
into the possibility of tomorrow.

Jane Sudworth

A Blue Ribbon at Amesbury

Such a fine pullet ought to go
All coiffured to a winter show
And be exhibited, and win.
The answer to this one has been –

And come with all her honors home.
Her golden leg, her coral comb,
Her fluff of plumage, white as chalk,
Her style, were all the fancy's talk.

It seems as if you must have heard.
She scored an almost perfect bird.
In her we make ourselves acquainted
With one a Sewell might have painted.

Here common with the flock again,
At home in her abiding pen,
She lingers feeding at the trough,
The last to let night drive her off.

The one who gave her ankle-band,
Her keeper, empty pail in hand,
He lingers too, averse to slight
His chores for all the wintry night.

He leans against the dusty wall,
Immured almost beyond recall,
A depth past many swinging doors,
And many litter-muffled floors.

He meditates the breeder's art.
He has a half a mind to start,
With her for Mother Eve, a race
That shall all living things displace.

'Tis ritual for her to lay
The full six days, then rest a day;
At which rate barring broodiness,
She may well score an egg success.

The gatherer can always tell
Her well-turned egg's brown shapely shell,
As safe a vehicle of seed
As is vouchsafed to feathered breed.

No human specter at the feast
Can scant or hurry her the least.
She takes her time to take her fill.
She whets a sleepy sated bill.

She gropes across the pen alone
To peck herself a precious stone.
She waters at the patent fount.
And so to roost, the last to mount.

The roost is her extent of flight.
Yet once she rises to the height,
She shoulders with a wing so strong
She makes the whole flock move along.

The night is setting in to blow.
It scours the windowpane with snow,
But barely gets from them or her
For comment a complacent chirr.

The lowly pen is yet a hold
Against the dark and wind and cold
To give a prospect to a plan
And warrant prudence in a man.

Robert Frost (1874 – 1963)

On A Cock At Rochester

Thou Cursed Cock, with thy perpetual Noise,
May'st thou be Capon made, and lose thy Voice,
Or on a Dunghil may'st thou spend thy Blood,
And Vermin prey upon thy craven Brood;
May Rivals tread thy Hens before thy Face,
Then with redoubled Courage give thee chase;
May'st thou be punish'd for *St Peter's* Crime,
And on *Shrove-tuesday*, perish in thy Prime;
May thy bruised Carcass be some Beggar's Feast,
Thou first and worst Disturber of Man's Rest.

Sir Charles Sedley (1639 – 1701)

Fingers in the Nesting Box

My heart would be faithless
If ever I forgot
My farmhouse adventure
One day by the fowl run
When Phoebe (of the fringe
And the fairy-story face)
Incited me to forage
Under speckled feathers
For the first time.

Fabulous I thought it,
Fabulous and fateful
(Before familiarity
With the fond pastime
My feelings blunted),
To clasp in frightened fingers
A firm, warm, round ...
'Phoebe, dear Phoebe,
What have I found?'

Robert Graves (1895 – 1985)

Scrambled

it's dark   don't like the dark
sing a song make the dark go away
look what they've done to my song, Ma
lalalalalalala must've done wrong
bad egg   cracked egg   smacksmacksmack
poor egg   poor hen   Humpty Dumpty Dad
in bits and pieces all the King's horses
and all the King's men can't put Humpty
together again   "puir wee hen" says Humpty
when baby stumbles and tumbles   when the bough
breaks   puir wee hen when when when will you lay
me an egg for my tea? Not a stone egg   Silly
hen   Bad hen   smacksmack   sticks and stones
will break my bones   chop off her head.
The blood's all red
Look what they've done to my brain, Ma
They've picked it like a chicken-bone
and chickchickchickchick chicken Run quick
cradle's falling Ma   catch Baby Bunting
fetch Daddy   Daddy's gone a hunting somebody
catch her too late can't put her together
again   say something
Bye Baby Bunting   bye baby   baby doesn't
like the dark   sing song make dark go away

Jacqueline Brown (1944 – 2008)

Doubt

A chick has just so much time
to chip its way out, just so much
egg energy to apply to the weakest spot
or whatever spot it started at.
It can't afford doubt. Who can?
Doubt uses albumen
at twice the rate of work.
One backward look by any of us
can cost what it cost Orpheus.
Neither may you answer
the stranger's knock;
you know it is the Person from Porlock
who eats dreams for dinner,
his napkin stained the most delicate colors.

Kay Ryan

Untitled

And here they are, healthy and plump
in excellent condition and, when they feel
like it, capable of producing
some excellent results.

They also believe they are by rights
entitled to massacre shrubs, bulbs
and flower beds, to terrify our aged cat
and peck on doors and windows

demanding bacon rinds, berries,
Tarte Tatin, granary bread, jumbo oats,
bagels, salmon scraps,
and goats' cheese quiche.

Ruthless, they squawk and cluck
dropping crap on lawn and deck.
Despite our telling them
how lucky they are

they show no gratitude at all.

Diana Gittins

March Araucana

Her feathers blow backwards
but she hops out
onto a stone and sips
pondwater. Frogspawn
ripples in the gusts.
She tips up her head.
Her bright comb's
a first flower.

Jean Atkin

Cock before dawn

Those dabbing hens I ferociously love
sag on their perches, half deflated.
I'll have none of it. I'm regimental. A plumbline
goes from my head to my toes. I burnish
the dark with my breast.

Lucifer's my blood brother. When I spread my wings
I'm crystal battlements and thunderbolts. I tread the earth
by pretending not to.

The West and the East are measured from me …
It's time I crowed. The sun will be waiting.

Norman MacCaig (1910 – 1996)